Finding.

Fran Francis

Foreword by John Otway

To [...] Best Wishes Fran (handwritten inscription)

Bank House Books

by the same author

non fiction

Bereavement Without Death

Finding Space

Profits from the sale of this book will be donated to SPACE, a project based at St Mary's Church, Aylesbury which aims to support people who are coping with the break-down of a close personal relationship.

First published 1999

Copyright © Fran Francis

All rights reserved.

British Library Cataloguing in Publication Data

A catalogue record for this book is available from the British Library

ISBN 0 9534119 1 5

Published by Bank House Books,
Box No. 20, St Mary's Church,
St Mary's Square, Aylesbury,
Bucks HP20 1JJ

Printed and bound in Great Britain by
Chalfont Bookbinders & Printers
The National Society for Epilepsy
Chalfont St Peter
Bucks SL9 0RJ

Cover photograph by
Robert Taylor, LBIPP LMPA

Contents

Foreword by John Otway

1

Needing Space	3
The Invitation	4
Another New Year	5
Homely Peace	6
Forgiveness	7
First Day of Term	8
Gifts For The Grieving	9
Hurrying	10
My Child	11
To An Adolescent Daughter	12
Letting Go	14
Certainty	15
Winter Loneliness	16
A Thought	18

2

A Different Child	21
A Difficult Perspective	22
Maturity	24
Candle Light	25
Autumn	26
Awareness	27
A Snow Shower in Spring	28
Spring	29
Waiting	30
Answers	31
A New Direction	32
A Way of Life	34
Parting	35
A Moment in Time	36
The First Day	37

Words	38
A Special Life	39
Awaiting Results	40

3

Loss of Trust	43
In Memory	44
Consequences	46
Facing The Truth	47
Loneliness	48
To Love And To Cherish	49
Disillumination	50
A Special Day	51
Miss Marple	52
Supporters	53
Death By Anger	54
Dreams And Reality	55
No Lighted Candle	56
Happy Days	58
Evening Dream	59
For Luke – With Hope	60

4

A Silent Scream	63
A Road For Helen	64
Spring Sunshine	66
Helplessness	67
It Is Difficult	68
Learning Just To Be	69
Electricity	70
The Fish Pond	71
Love	72
Feeling Alone	73
Hopes And Dreams	74
Weather	75
Distancing	76
It Doesn't End Here	77
Rudge	78
Time To Move On	79
Finding Space	80

Foreword

I managed with a large degree of success over the years to fulfil the role of a horrid and embarrassing younger brother to my sister. However, with marriage came the opportunity of changing surname and so Fran was able to, and presumably did, regularly deny all connection with me.

She must have watched with a certain degree of helpless alarm as I pupated from spotty adolescent into fully grown punk rocker, something at which I was reasonably adept and I relentlessly courted as much publicity as I could.

This was not to be just a phase in growing up. Our mother always felt I would end up getting a proper job like the rest of the family had, my four sisters grew into three nurses and a social worker. But with me, the punk rock embarrassment continues to the present day.

I therefore marvel at Fran's kindness in asking me to write something as a foreword to her first poetry book. Not that we haven't had much contact, far from it, Fran has had the privilege of putting the whole band and road crew up in her house when we've been touring.

Maybe it's just that she has the rare ability to see enough redeeming features in her brother to forgive the prodigal sibling, maybe it's because during her time as a social worker she came across sisters who had even more embarrassing younger brothers or possibly the experience of bringing up a family leaves one immune to this sort of thing.

Whatever, It's an honour to kick the book off and if what I've just written sounds a little flippant for a book of thoughtful work, it's just that I'm not a suitable person to write intelligently about poetry. It's also, in my view, preferable to let the poems stand up for themselves and enjoy them for what they mean to you without younger brother spoiling it all.

Although the stuff I've done has been confined to penning pop songs, I have enjoyed the writing I've done and I really hope that Fran has that same sort of genuine pleasure out of the creative process and the rewards it brings.

You choose your friends and are given your family. On the big birthday when the gifts of family are given, I would compare the presents thus; with me, Fran got a woolly jersey knitted by an Aunt Flora with an interesting taste in colour and pattern and with Fran, I got a really neat Apple Macintosh computer with infinite amounts of RAM - that I not only love a lot but also find very useful.

I trust that you will get a great deal of enjoyment from her work I'm sure you will.

John Otway

Part 1

NEEDING SPACE

The chaos in my head,
whirling, turning, moving, changing,
so much to do,
what to do next?

Not enough hours in the day,
if there were more,
I wouldn't have the energy
to cope with them.

I want time and space
to sort out where and what is me,
to try to discover what I want
and what I want to do.

A precious few minutes space
grabbed and savoured with a coffee,
sufficed to keep things ticking over
for a long, long time.

But now, constantly coping, super person,
always available, there on demand,
wants some space
and a life of her own.

THE INVITATION

Moments after the invitation is opened,
anxiety begins to disperse the euphoria,
the question and the mood begin to show,
"what on earth am I going to wear?"

For some this is the beginning
of an exciting game called
'seek the elusive, perfect outfit',
the function -
the place to display success.

For others it is the chance to wear
a special outfit rarely worn
or an opportunity to justify
the "just have to have it"
or an earlier impulse buy.

For many, the enjoyment is evasive,
standing in the middle of the bedroom,
surrounded by heaps of rejected clothes,
the panic in the voice rises,
"I'll never find something to wear".

Trying to deal with the anxiety
and lessen the panic attacks,
such comments as
"this will do fine"
as submerged garments are discovered
and held up for inspection or
"what about the one you bought …?"
can damage all but the strongest friendships.

But somehow, by whatever means,
in an outfit, rediscovered, bought or borrowed,
numerous people gather together,
to celebrate their recovery from the trauma of,
"what on earth am I going to wear."

ANOTHER NEW YEAR

New Years Day,
start of another year.
Yet again,
this one is going to be different.

But somehow I know it is.
All the other attempts
that didn't quite make it,
just like giving up smoking,
heap up,
until they build success.

It's all too easy
to see the attempts
that didn't quite make it
as failures,
rather than trial runs,
practices,
for the real thing.

HOMELY PEACE

The noises in the house
waft upward to my room;
a TV showing a soap,
a stereo playing heavy metal,
a computer game jangling
its' characters to death.

Sitting quietly, feeling apart,
trying to find the quiet
in my own room,
in my own space,
allowing my mind to wander,
I try to think.

The sound of laughing voices
do not disturb,
they signal 'all is well',
then sounds of bickering intrude,
bringing me back annoyed,
needing to intervene.

A snarling yelp of
"what you doing?" suffices.
The expected response of "nothing,"
brings back the calm,
allowing the noisy quiet
to continue its peacefulness.

FORGIVENESS

You said
you would never let go
of your anger and pain,
to do this would let him go.

You said
if you were happy
and had a life,
he would feel it's OK.

You said
you were going to
hang on to your misery,
to punish him.

You said
one day you would make him
realise what he had done,
then he would hurt.

But the sad thing is,
you are punishing you,
giving control of your life to him.

Holding on to your anger and pain,
you give him the centre of your life,
around which you revolve.

Hard though it is,
to forgive and let go,
you would be giving yourself
the gift of your life.

FIRST DAY OF TERM

Yesterday, school bags were checked,
old notes were found
giving parents late information,
unfinished homework discovered,
along with a lack of pens, pencils and paper.
The bottom of the bag was rediscovered,
probably for the first time in months,
then carefully repacked
for the last time this term.

As clothes and bags were checked,
the wail of parenthood arose in many homes,
"why didn't you tell me before that –
you have no pencils,"
"your shoes are too tight,"
"why wasn't that done before?"
"what have you done with them?"
"why didn't you put it in the wash?"
"thank goodness it's school tomorrow."

This morning the alarm insists
that normality has returned,
households echo to the sounds of -
"will you get out of bed!"
"hurry up!"
"I don't want to go to school,"
"I can't find my ...."
the organisation of the day before
rarely fulfills its promises.

Now, both house and street are quiet,
recuperating from the onslaught of the holiday.
The mess in the house
quietly waits for order to be restored.
For a few moments,
a pause in life's merry-go-round
and a cup of coffee can be grabbed,
before facing the washing up
and the rest of life.

GIFTS FOR THE GRIEVING

The gift of a touch,
from someone who cares,
to give me warmth.

The gift of time,
from someone willing
just to be with me.

The gift of listening,
enabling me to open
and free my heart.

The gift of allowing
me to be me, to deal with this
in my own way.

The gift of not judging,
not heaping up reassurances
or confusing my brain with advice.

The gift of restraint,
in what you say to others
of how I was or what I said.

The gift of staying power,
my loss is for always,
recovery will take a while.

The gift of a helping hand,
when life's simple necessities
feel like a mountain to climb.

The gift of ordinaryness,
life goes on whilst I am out of it,
people living, laughing, crying,
remind me it is still there
and that one day I will rejoin it.

HURRYING

I wish I hadn't hurried so much,
where was I going? What for?
Time gained was self lost
in the stress and strain of getting there.

Trying to catch up, where should I be?
What's been forgotten? What can't I see?
Trying to make up for the things I felt missing,
trying to fill the emotional gaps.

The sad thing is, when looking back,
most of it didn't matter.
The things of importance at the time,
each changed and gave us very little.

Other people coped much better,
calmer and managing they seemed to be,
feeling a failure, inadequate and stupid,
I could not see many felt like me.

Tired, I tried to find the site,
where coping, space and ease are found,
not knowing this is placed within,
bowed I sought it from without.

Your face looked stressed as you hurried along
cross and tugging at your child,
"there's no time now for fun and play,
perhaps there'll be time another day."

Our feelings, our sense and questioning,
Whose life? What's important? What for?
must have importance, time and care
or we lose ourselves whilst getting there.

MY CHILD

You borrowed the car.
You who were my baby,
my toddler,
my child,
a moment ago.

You borrowed my life
whilst you grew –

then you gave it back
and found your own.

My life has a well worn patch,
soft and cosy like a well loved toy,
kept for comfort when the world is hard
on my baby,
my toddler,
my child,
of a moment ago.

TO AN ADOLESCENT DAUGHTER

I wonder if you will ever know,
how much I love you.
Love can't be seen,
love can't be measured,
how can I show it to you?

At your age,
it is difficult to tell,
whether you realise,
whether you don't
or whether you ever will.

One day you may have
children of your own.
Will you feel
the same about them,
as I feel about my own?

My love gives boundaries
which you love to hate.
My love makes me moan,
my love makes me nag,
homework, curfews, what a drag.

We never agree
what each other should wear.
Compromise is difficult,
we both often swear
but we usually work it out.

I hope for you,
I wish for you,
but all I can really do
is stand back and be there,
in case I am needed.

If you know I am here,
if you know that I will listen,
that I will try to understand
and always be there for you,
then perhaps you do know.

LETTING GO

To be able to let go,
first,
we must understand,
what it is we are holding on to.

To move on,
first,
we must want to.

CERTAINTY

All too often,
just when you're sure
you know what you're doing,
just when you're sure
you've got it cracked,
just when you're sure
you understand,
it all goes wrong
or falls apart
or you find to your horror
you've been mistaken –
but –
now and then
if we keep trying,
often after gaining
a little modesty,
we gain the prize
of success.

WINTER LONELINESS

Feeling her aloneness
like the walls of her house, surrounding her,
she put on her coat.
Trying to leave
the loneliness behind, she left the house
to look for hope.

She looked around
and saw the urban landscape was showing
signs of spring.
The warm sun
giving a feeling of impending greenness,
lifted her spirits.

A man gardening
greeted her with a cheery "good morning"
and a smile.
Returning the greeting,
she felt her smile as it began to soften her face
and light her eyes.

Walking towards her,
two boys scuffing their way home from school
grinned at her.
Smiling she thought,
'what a scruffy lot this younger generation are,
but
some are nice.'

As she went,
she greeted a toddler, out walking
with his mother.
She chatted
to a neighbour, out enjoying the fresh air
with her dog.

Then back home,
with all the smiles and greetings she had
collected
to give her comfort,
sitting dozing,
grey head drooping, warmed by the fire,
she smiled.

A THOUGHT

Inheritors of the knowledge
of what is right and what is wrong,
have been given free will
to choose the way they live.

Part 2

A DIFFERENT CHILD

His face was close on the TV screen
but he did not look out,
his view was inward to his pain,
lines of grief were etched on his face.

He talked flatly about his little son
and the loss of the joy of his birth.
"Why were we the chosen ones?
Why did this happen to us?"

Suddenly his life had changed forever,
turned upside down and inside out.
Expectation, fulfilment, happiness, vanished,
with grief, resentment, confusion, replaced.

Many months of "Why?" have passed
but the feelings fresh as on that day,
grieve the father every time
he gazes on his laughing son.

A DIFFICULT PERSPECTIVE

You stood there telling me,
about your friends' new baby,
about its' parents distress
because of the mark on his face.

My thoughts raced on
looking for a suitable response,
whilst my feelings, divided in two
robbed me of coherent words.

"Oh" was all I managed to mumble,
as the two sides of my internal debate
fought for supremacy or balance,
looking back both sides were right.

I was sorry for the parents
who were denied a perfect child,
who, whilst living with the difference
will search for a cure or normal life.

Sorry for the child
coping with his difference
in an often cruel, rejecting world
or facing pain to look like others.

But I also wanted to say,
"Is that all? Be happy with the child,
this is such a minor thing,
of no great problem whatsoever."

For him a life, like any other;
friends, career, marriage and children.
He can choose whatever he wishes,
so many of these are denied my brother.

Though speech is restored, I can't explain.
If I said how sad, I would also need to say,
"I know well, it could be so much worse,"
but as a father to be, you don't need this.

MATURITY?

Naïve beyond my years,
faced with the wisdom of innocence,
I fail to understand what I had known,
when I had innocence of my own.

CANDLE LIGHT

The candle flickers,
its' tiny, humble light, like hope,
shines brightly in the gloom.

Its tiny power,
connecting people and generations
drawn to its enigmatic, mysterious light.

Light of remembrance,
light of celebration,
light of prayer and contemplation.

Softly and gently,
essential light of so many for so long,
touches mood and thought.

No stark electric power and light,
speed, precision and accuracy,
giving no flicker or dancing shadows.

Fragile life
needing air, shelter, food and care,
to keep the light alive.

Light for remembrance,
of those other lights
now gone.

Light for awareness,
of the scant life and light
of many.

Light for the mind,
that we may see more clearly
the light that we've been given.

AUTUMN

Autumn arrived too soon,
it feels like winter,
whilst I still wish
for a few more weeks of summer.

I am not ready
to be here where I am,
in the year, in my life.

I am not asking to go back,
just wishing,
for a little more summer.

AWARENESS

We tend to be aware of how much
people do not listen
when we need someone to listen to us.

We tend to forget that each person
sees life from a different perspective
when we are not understood.

We are aware of others rushing in
with answers, platitudes and generalisations
when these are inappropriate to us.

Rarely do we remember
how much these things upset and hurt us,
when we do it to others.

If we can allow ourselves to learn,
if we can allow ourselves
to be out of the picture for a few moments,
if we can listen to and hear another,
we may be surprised to discover
that what we learn about is ourselves.

A SNOW SHOWER IN SPRING

Suddenly we were back in winter again
when we had almost reached summer.
All had gone quiet,
except for the sound of cars
slushing their way down the street.

Though the snow quickly melted,
it lingered for a moment,
the touch of winter on the blossoms.

It stopped and disappeared
as quickly as it came,
blueness again spread across the sky,
birds sang again as they resumed
feeding and teaching their young.

Though reminders of the past appear,
one snow shower does not mean
we have gone back to winter.

SPRING

Spring is arriving step by step,
though some trees are still bare,
others are covered in blossom,
the promise of fruit to come.

The beauty of Spring
has transformed,
is transforming
the landscape,
changing shape and colour.

When it has fulfilled its task
it will disappear,
taking blossom and daffodils with it,
giving way,
allowing summer to blend into being.

When does Spring arrive?
With the first crocus,
the beginning of March
or the warmer weather?
And when does it go?

When is our own Spring?
when we are young,
when life has renewed us or
are there endless new possibilities?

Perhaps we, like the landscape,
however old, have within us
all that is needed for another Spring,
just waiting for the touch of the sun.

WAITING

The little face shone with eager anticipation,
early morning, bag packed,
she sat on the stairs,
watching the door,
waiting for Daddy to come.

Time crept on
trepidation grew,
"come and play,"
"no I'm waiting here
for Daddy to come."

"You must be hungry,
come and have some lunch,"
"I'll wait here for Daddy,
he will be hungry too,
when he comes."

"Darling come and wait in here,
draw him a picture,
have a play,"
"no I'll wait here so I'll be ready,
to go and play with him."

"Perhaps he cannot come today,
come and have some tea,"
"I'm really not hungry
he'll be here soon,
he promised he'd come today."

Bedtime, hope gone,
heartache holding heartbreak,
trying to comfort the tear-filled sobs,
knowing the question,
searching for the answer,
"Why Mummy, why, didn't he come?"

ANSWERS

Our children have many questions
and look to us for the answers,
which often we do not have.

When we can admit this to them
and they can accept it from us,
we can go searching together.

A NEW DIRECTION

It will always be better when –
the exams are over,
I have the right job,
my own home,
a bigger income,
the children are grown –

But better rarely has its day,
overtaken by the next event,
the waiting starts all over again.

Now never seems possible,
manageable, affordable,
it always remains in the future,
"perhaps in a while,"
"we will when we can."

Suddenly,
too much of life has gone,
waited away,
and there's still so much to wait for,
large and small,
"when I've dusted,"
"when we have the money,"
"when we have the time."

For some,
the day comes when the light dawns,
the reasons cease to make sense,
stopping to think,
this is my life I'm living.
Grasping life in order to live it,
not assuming an endless future,
not equating money with happiness,
financial security with inner peace.

Looking at the rat race,
changing priorities,
seeing the sacrifices as well as the gains,
calming the doubts,
ignoring the doubters –
the dreadful mistake they think you're making!

My life is now,
this is not a rehearsal.

A WAY OF LIFE

Sometimes it seems a pity,
when the world seems cruel and harsh,
you will not be allowed to stay,
the sweet innocent you could always be.

Yet in another mood I see,
the world has the world to offer,
then I regret the things
you will never know and do.

If you are distressed or hurt,
I am distressed and hurt too.
Wanting to keep you safe,
I impose my limitations,
by failing to see the obvious,
this is about me, not about you.

If you are not given challenges,
you will not have successes.
If you are not stretched,
you will feel no growth.
If you are not given independence,
you will experience no freedom.
Where there are no risks,
there can be no gains.
If sadness is avoided,
many joys will be missed.
Without risking loss,
there will be no love.

I must be brave,
to allow you courage.
Give you the love
and space you need
to explore and find a life
that you can fully live.

PARTING

I want to be quiet
and spend time on my own,
but I hate you having to leave.

Once goodbyes are said
and you have gone,
I miss you but I am content where I am.

Enjoying the tranquillity,
space and peace,
I look forward to the time
when we can be together again.

A MOMENT IN TIME

It was strange,
watching you all go off together,
all my children in my car,
independent of me.

The happy sad feelings
sat confused inside,
whilst I made a half-hearted attempt
to use the time, whilst awaiting your return.

How recently it seems
there'd be no agreement on the film seen,
disagreement in the car
and no-way would you be seen together.

The warmth of this moment
will not be diminished by its impermanence,
my role and life have also altered,
over all and on a day to day basis.

All of you together
joining smiles at my "be careful",
leave a snap-shot for my memory album
to keep for when you all go away.

THE FIRST DAY

Asleep
but tossing and turning,
calling out,
as the night fears,
in surreal action,
play through until morning.

Watching, listening,
re-visiting those nights when
I too had lain awake for hours
only to drop into troubled sleep,
with morning bringing
relief from the night and
dread of the day ahead.

Quiet, tired, rejecting breakfast,
feeling sick, wide eyed,
"how do I look?"
the new clothes look smart,
confident,
the shoulders straighten,
hesitation,
a purposeful step over the threshold,
into a new day.

WORDS

Sticks and stones may break my bones,
but others will care for me whilst they mend,
medicaments and sympathy gently applied,
whilst I am assured, all are on my side.

The hurt caused by words is rarely seen,
it is hidden, isolates and avoids attention,
weeping and festering in silent heartache,
no comfort or soothing to make it alright.

Silent hurt, running deep and wide,
can fill up all the space inside,
drowning love and happiness,
reducing life to less and less.

Words of healing, acts of caring,
stem the tide and ease the grief,
words have power to hurt or heal
and shape the way we live and feel.

A SPECIAL LIFE

You were with us for such a short time,
now before we are ready,
while there was still so much living to do,
death has taken you away.

You left us before we had the chance
to really know you,
before we could teach you what we know,
but you had already taught us so much.

Your life showed us a different life,
a way to see and value what we have,
many sadnesses and challenges we faced,
but none as great as this.

Our love for you goes with you
and goes on,
your love and all that you gave us
we keep.

We will cherish your life
and all we have learned,
in the life without you,
we now will live.

AWAITING RESULTS

The sun is shining,
there's so much to do,
but all I can do is sit and wait.

Await the decisions and opinions of others,
wait to know the results of the tests,
wait to see more of my future unfolding,
in semi-hope and semi-dread.

There are ramifications and likelihoods,
it's hard to know how well I did,
what they want, or what they found,
it all goes round inside my head.

How soon will I know?
Can I cope with the answer?
Will it be definite or just the next step?
It's scary and stupid to contemplate,
so much of my future in a 'no' or a 'yes'.

Trying to get on but I can't get on,
most of my being can only wait,
filling in time, awaiting results,
to give direction for what to do next.

Part 3

LOSS OF TRUST

It is strange,
that if I asked you
and you said "no",
I would still
not know the answer.

If you said "yes",
I would believe,
but,
would I want to hear –
the explanations,
the reasons,
the excuses?

Do I want to know?
Yes and no.
If I ask will I really know?
Can I face the upset
there will be,
from asking the question?
Whatever the answer.

It is lonely here,
knowing what might happen,
but,
not knowing what to do.

IN MEMORY

She was tired,
tired of caring,
of hearing others
and responding to their needs,
whilst no-one heard or helped her.

It was a heart attack they said,
very sudden,
no one expected it,
no-one had heard
the tired cries for help,
from the soft, warm heart they leaned on.

"What will we do now?"
"Who will we turn to?"
"How will we cope?"
"I can't,"
"you will have to,"
"I will do this, you must do that."

So many people
madly rushing about,
feeling pressed and over-stretched,
trying to do,
what one did quietly and unnoticed.

The realisation, too late,
"we should have done more,"
"she didn't say,"
"she didn't ask."
Vision clearing in retrospect,
"she hadn't looked happy for a while,"
"she was tired and short of breath."

The excuses pour,
her role is filled by rotas,
relatives, nurses, carers, services.

Many tears,
much regret,
too late to learn these lessons
and put the clock back.
This loss is forever.

CONSEQUENCES

No-one can cry that many tears
without changing,
no-one can cry that many tears
without moving on.
The place, time and person
are changed forever,
there can be no going back.

The tears dried,
the lessons learned,
the old view becomes dimmer
as perception changes,
with the angle of the view.

Later, in a different time and place,
the tears long dried,
the pangs mild and occasional,
memory fixes the time
as a life marker,
all life happened before or after
the event.

FACING THE TRUTH

How many times have I
climbed over my misgivings?
How many times have I
made excuses or offered explanations?
How many times have I
not accepted what was being said,
or made assumptions
about what was meant?

I now know
I was not ready to see
or face the truth.
Unable to consider inner doubts,
they were rapidly explained
and chased away.

I said and believed,
that I didn't know,
but looking back
with painful honesty,
I now realise,
I couldn't face knowing.

LONELINESS

Loneliness
is a resounding silence among the noise,
emphasised by those around not touching
with hand, deed, word or look.

How can I reach out
when I know it is my loneliness
reaching out like leper's hands.
I feel others cringing back,
sorry,
but afraid of being contaminated.

The lonely carry warnings
in their body language,
or in their efforts to hide their feelings.

Yet there are still those,
who see the need behind the façade,
who are secure and know
they will not be contaminated or engulfed,
who freely give, knowing
they will not lose part of themselves,
who know who and what they are
and know the value of the gifts they give,
the gift of contact, in a smile or kind word,
the gift of time,
the gift of caring in a careless world.

TO LOVE AND CHERISH

Meeting.
Togetherness joining us
'till death us do part'
and it did.

A life we had together,
making a future and a history.

Then the first death,
slowly and gradually
the you I knew left,
only to be glimpsed
in lucid moments and in sleep,
gradually disappearing until
even the body shell
became hardly recognisable.

Giving my love
to the memory of your love.
My caring,
to the memory of promises made.
I kept you but lost you.

But my love could not hold you,
my care could not stay
the second death,
freeing you to be whole
in another place,
freeing me from my service,
to be alone.

DISILLUMINATION

To have a life we must live a life,
not things we have or what others say,
holding on, not moving on,
we face stagnation and death in life.

By giving up babyhood a toddler emerges,
the longing to grow is strong and sure,
for a while crawling back is a warm possibility
but once on this road there is no turning back.

Profound is the drive for freedom and growth,
no thought is given for what's left behind,
we measure, assess and encourage them onward,
forgetting through them the life that we lack.

All the child sees are freedoms, horizons,
keen to move on, discounting the risks,
facing and coping with bumps and frustrations,
their view of the world is bright and fresh.

Keen eyed and questioning, full of energy,
our children are what we used to be,
given our hindsight, learning and knowledge,
we show them the dimmed world, we see it to be.

A SPECIAL DAY

It was a pity that Mum
was too busy to come,
the day I was a bridesmaid.

I wore a pink dress,
looked like a princess,
with shoes of shiny satin.

A shirt with ruffles
and shoes with buckles,
my brother, a page boy wore.

The bride dressed in cream,
looked just like a dream,
her groom was a handsome prince.

It's such a pity my Mum
was too busy to come,
the day my Dad married Jane.

MISS MARPLE

I like the idea of Miss Marple
an elderly, spinsterish, villagey lady
of sharp wit.

Not travelled but cosmopolitan,
all seeing with apparently little to see
in the village.

An understanding of the microcosm
and the macrocosm it represents
but appearing dithery.

Travel broadens the mind but
not necessarily giving more insight
than a walk down the lane.

Experience and understanding gained
is experience and understanding gained
where ever from.

External appearances are misleading,
wit, depth and a cunning mind can be hidden
behind knitting, specs and a country hat.

SUPPORTERS

We sat there together
we three,
you two listening to me

flanked either side
by warmth,
touched by touch

the distance felt
far away,
the closeness close

a shoulder for a head
a hand for a hand,
support given

talking through the muddle
and fears,
seeking clarity

DEATH BY ANGER

An unhappy man
making himself unhappier,
holding on to anger and pain,
lost hopes, lost fears
and memories of camaraderie
in the war.

He could have achieved something
but for:
his wife, the child, lack of support,
being apprenticed by his father
to the wrong trade, a lifetime ago.

Talents remaining unrecognised,
his frustration seethed angrily,
his resentment coldly fumed.
Controlled by his own firm routines
he expected from his wife,
meat and two veg
at twelve thirty.

Turned outward and inward
anger alienating, isolating, controlling,
damaging body and mind.
Facing no fighting in wartime,
facing no peace in peacetime,
he died of anger injuries
to the heart.

DREAMS AND REALITY

The emptiness inside
draws me inwards,
trying to fill the space
where love should be.

The load I carry
on my shoulders
weighs me down.
Where is my help?

Looking in,
looking down,
wishing
for the unknown warmth
of imagined love.

Rejecting
the longed for but
unrecognised touch,
reality rarely looks
like we dreamed it.

NO LIGHTED CANDLE

If you had died,
I could have laid in my cold and lonely bed,
thinking of you in your colder and harsher grave.

I would have thought of you,
forced to leave when you wanted to stay.
No more a part of our daily lives,
no more able to share in the joys and sorrows,
as it used to be.

But,
there would have been words of condolence,
letters, cards and flowers.

There would have been a service,
people together in love, care and grief.

I could have chosen the hymns,
the ones I know,
the ones I would remember and sing,
to remember the care and love that day.

Perhaps I would see you cradled in the arms of God,
perhaps I would believe or feel you near me
and would talk to you as I used.

Then keeping all the love and good things you gave,
I would let you go,
to follow your new life in a place I cannot yet be,
but one day I would share with you.

I would have mourned you long and hard
because I loved you.

But,

you lie in a warm and friendly bed,
not taken from us, you just walked away,
able but refusing to share the joys and sorrows,
as it used to be.

Not condolences but questions.
No flowers, no cards but a letter saying "what happened?
For the best? Or should we be sorry?"

There was no service,
no coming together of love and support,
no hymns.

I know in whose arms you are cradled,
I feel you near me when you collect the kids
and on the phone we talk,
but not as we used.

I let you go,
I had no choice,
with no hope of reunion in that other place,
I mourned you long and hard
because I loved you.

HAPPY DAYS

Somewhere around here,
somewhere along this road
I believe I was told
I would find happy ever after.

Being realistic I knew
childhood days are not the happiest,
early days of career and marriage
are stressful times
and children create problems.

Marriages end,
children grow up and leave
and happy ever after
is just around the corner.

EVENING DREAM

Darkness falls on another day,
time to put the kids away,
leave for tomorrow
chores still undone,
sit down and relax
evening has come.

FOR LUKE - WITH HOPE

I feel I have no roots,
as they grew someone kept pulling them up
because they said they were wrong.

I do not have my things
because they said they were unlovely or no use
and made me give them away.

I feel I have nothing
because they tell me it all belongs to someone else.

I do not have me
because someone kept telling me I was all wrong
and threw the parts away.

I still have my feelings,
my anger, my apologies and my fears.

They punish me for my feelings,
they beat me for my anger,
they bask in my apologies
and rule me with my fears.

With no roots I have lived,
so I know I can live and need not fear.
I am free – to search and find me,
to leave this vacuum and find a space that's mine.

There I will find me – the me I truly am,
I will grow roots to plant where I wish,
I will have things that I want
and things that I need – to keep if I wish.

One day, my feelings,
my anger, my apologies and my fears
will have their place in the armoury of my life,
alongside new feelings of love,
happiness and hope.

Part 4

A SILENT SCREAM

How many decibels are there
in a silent scream?
Enough to deafen the screamer
and damage their thoughts.

How much damage is created
by the earthquake of loss?
No points on the richter scale,
but a life is totally devastated.

Watching in deaf terror as people pass
unaware of shaken earth and casualties,
there is a sudden realisation,
life has moved to a parallel universe.

For them nothing has happened,
there is no cacophony of confusion,
getting on with getting on,
they are not aware of the new arrival.

Not aware of the aching wail,
the wish for the comfort and security
of the time before the scream and the quake,
a wish for the impossible, to go back.

A ROAD FOR HELEN

All my life I have been heading
down this road,
its taken me all my life
to get here.

I have worked so very hard
to be where I am,
I have given up so much
to achieve all this.

When the going got tough
I was there,
unsupported and against the odds
I saw it through.

At last all the effort was worthwhile,
security was gained,
there may not be love, care and support
but I have what I have.

There was always the possibility and hope
that things would change,
that having given so much of myself
I would be rewarded.

But suddenly all that had seemed secure
has gone,
all that had been worked for
has gone.

How many times have I fought the odds
and kept going?
I was too sure, frightened and had given too much
to let it go.

I could not forsee or believe this end
in my wildest dreams,
this is what happens to other people
who have failed.

Have I really reached the end
of this road?
I want to keep going, I am not ready yet
to let it go.

What should I do? No doubt there are other roads
if I look around,
but for once I will sit and think for a while
before I move on.

SPRING SUNSHINE

The bright spring sunshine
lifts spirit and mood
whilst showing up dust
and dirty windows.
The urge to spend time in the garden,
out in the countryside
or anywhere away from the house,
becomes very strong.

HELPLESSNESS

"It's your decision,
I can do nothing.
You will decide what you want
in your own time
and I can do nothing about it.

You know what I want,
I've told you so often
but you can't decide
what you want to do
and I can do nothing about it.

You say you are suffering,
feeling sorry for yourself
you think I should understand.
My feelings don't seem to matter
and I can do nothing about it.

You say you will decide soon,
you need more time and space,
that this is very difficult for you.
It is very difficult for me
and I can do nothing about it.

I can go or tell you to leave,
what I want is for you to stay.
Only you can decide
if you are willing to do that
and I can do nothing about it."

He slowly looked up,
"I have decided to do nothing,
I have chosen to give you choice,
to let you decide which step we take
because you are the one
who can do something about it."

IT IS DIFFICULT

It is hard
to let go of what we had,
to let go and sever the ties
to a person, place or thing,
to let go of waiting, hoping, wanting
and not to let go of the belief
that we still have something.

LEARNING JUST TO BE

My hurt and my pain are mine,
all that's left when all else is gone,
let me keep them for a while
to know and learn from them.

Don't try and rationalise them away,
explain them into extinction
or throw your answers at them
because they are uncomfortable for you.

Stay and just be or take your leave.
Allow me to understand,
to learn and grow from them,
then maybe there will be a point.

You cannot make it better,
only I can do that,
but a friend by my side
will help to ease the way.

ELECTRICITY

Checking the house late at night,
when everyone else has gone to bed.
In the dark, tiny lights glow,
power on duty whilst we sleep.

Green light on the freezer
shows coldness is maintained.
Red light on sockets and telephone,
ready and waiting for use.

Numbers on clocks and video recorders,
patiently counting time and life away
until the allotted, programmed hour,
when they burst into activity.

Power off means panic and stress,
no awakening, difficulty coping,
freezer defrosting, no kettle boiling,
how to manage 'til it's back on?

Reassuring, glowing lights,
give assurance that some things
are well, working and under control,
power on duty even while we sleep.

Power supplied by nature and man,
needed by and connecting us all,
enhancing life and creating dependency,
simplifying and complicating existence.

So as I wander around the house at night,
when everyone is fast asleep,
the lights give a sense of connection,
to many others, who are also awake.

THE FISH POND

Last year the water in the pond
remained green and cloudy,
I hardly saw the fish at all.

This year the water cleared
and the heron enjoyed the fish.

Now I have a fish tank
and a pretty bog garden.

LOVE

Love cannot be taught
or bought
it can only be given.

Learned by gift
but not in gifts,
they are tokens.

Binding with freedom,
an emotion
without sentimentality.

Power of gentleness,
invisible presence,
source and end.

FEELING ALONE

Feeling alone,
isolated from the world
but it seems
this is how too many feel.

Feeling different,
misunderstood by others,
it is easy
to withdraw into ourselves.

Feeling apart,
out of touch with life,
we can seem
solitary and detached.

Feeling contact,
reverses the spiral,
opening up
a door to the world.

HOPES AND DREAMS

Growing,
we dream our dreams.
Under life's realities they are tested,
then hidden, denied, discarded or kept.

Some dreams are shelved,
others replaced.
Looking like a different direction
failed dreams are replaced,
by the dreams they replaced.

Rejected and reclaimed,
these dreams have stood the test of time,
strong and vibrant,
they cannot be denied.

If we have dared to dream,
gentled fears, accepted losses
and renewed our dreams,
hope and optimism will closely follow.

Knowing more the value of our dreams,
never again will we give them up
for second best,
our own doubts,
or the urging of others.

Sadly parting from those
whose journey is along a different path,
we treasure those
whose journey is with us.

Then taking a more sure direction,
we travel the new
but well dreamed road
we found before and now re-discover.

WEATHER

Grey and overcast,
the weather fits my spirits.
Tears fall from the clouds
and the wind blows
in sob like gusts.

Gradually it calms.
Such weather,
like such times in our lives,
do not last forever
but while in the midst of it,
it may be impossible to believe
the sun will shine again.

DISTANCING

If I did not come again
would you notice?
Perhaps,
but would you let me stay away
without a "why" or "are you OK?"

Giving me a freedom I already own,
feels like uncaring.
Do I only imagine you care?

Within the silence and space
of correctness and unexpressed feelings,
where warmth and spontaneity
are naïve, uncool or threatening,
distance grows.

IT DOESN'T END HERE

It could be said
that this partnership had run its course,
but, like so many others
this partnership had become a way of life,
creating life that grew from and within it.

Had it run its course
whilst full of potential for dynamic growth?
Whilst still nurturing life and talent?
No,
a different life had beckoned,
the glitter of the new and exciting,
casting a shadow,
obscuring the view of the home scene.

'till death us do part'
became a discounted anachronism
and the 'sins of the fathers'
silently, unnoticed, crept in
to fulfil the prophesy.
Visiting grief, pain and unhappiness,
on the children
and the future generations.

RUDGE

Dear old dog,
as the life in you begins to fade,
hips stiffen, eyes and hearing begin to fail,
I dread the decision I may have to make.

I have become very fond of you
in the few years we have shared a house.
It is hard to remember a time
when you were not part of my life.

You have a sort of quiet dignity
that makes me question who is the better
and makes me question my role as master
and consider our place in each others' lives.

Asleep, you lie beside my desk,
less alert than before but always ready
to follow each time I leave the room,
keeping me near for protection.

When you go I will miss you a lot,
my only hope is that you will be allowed
to quietly slip into eternal sleep,
in the home that we both share.

TIME TO MOVE ON?

I was very involved in my past,
I was there,
I did my best,
I was hurt.

Out there is my future.

Dare I be involved in it?
Dare I be there?
Dare I give my best?
Dare I risk hurt?

What can I do?

I want to stay here,
confused and undecided.
I want to go back,
change the past and put it right.
I want to go forward
and make the future good.

I don't know how to do it,
I'm frightened.
Please can I just go back to bed?

FINDING SPACE

Looking for space in my life.
Time and space for me
to do what I want with no interruptions.
Where is it?

What do I have to do to find it?
Is it here or in another place?
What is the cost of having some time?
Who will pay?

Perhaps the place to start
is by handing responsibility back to each
for their own lives (plus washing and ironing).
This needs strength.

Perhaps there's gain in a business plan,
with strategic priorities, evaluations
and efficient deployment
of all my abilities.

Make lists, cut out unnecessaries –
how can I decide what these should be?
Do I really want to change my life
that much?

One day – who knows how far away,
when the house no longer resounds
with the chaos of family,
will I wish this time back?

How often do we have to lose things
before we realise their value to us
or become aware of the fleetingness
of this moment.